PICTURE LIBRARY

FOOTBALL

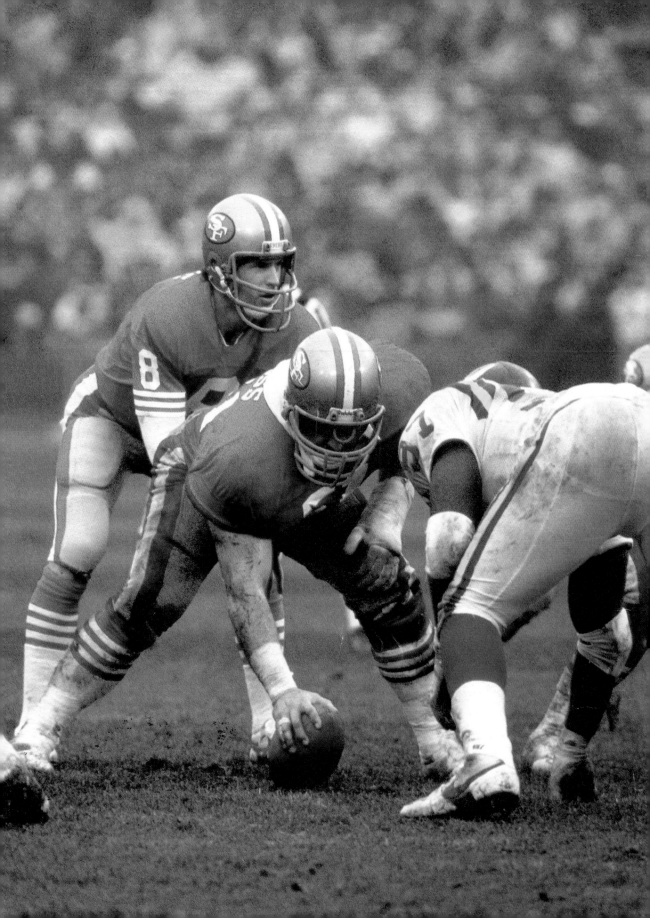

PICTURE LIBRARY
FOOTBALL

Norman Barrett

Franklin Watts

London   New York   Sydney   Toronto

© 1988 Franklin Watts Ltd

First published in Great Britain
    1988 by
Franklin Watts Ltd
12a Golden Square
London W1R 4BA

First published in the USA by
Franklin Watts Inc
387 Park Avenue South
New York
NY 10016

First published in Australia by
Franklin Watts
14 Mars Road
Lane Cove
NSW 2066

UK ISBN: 0 86313 685 0
US ISBN: 0-531-10632-2
Library of Congress Catalog Card
Number 88-50380

Printed in Italy

Designed by
Barrett & Willard

Photographs by
Action Plus
N.S. Barrett Collection

Illustrations by
Rhoda & Robert Burns

Technical Consultant
Nick Halling

Contents

Introduction

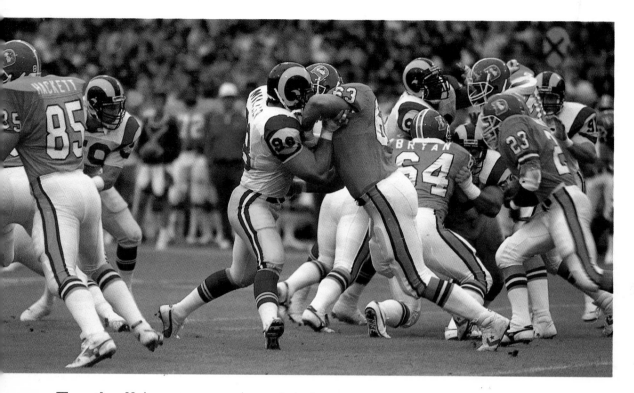

Football is a game in which two teams of eleven players aim to advance an oval ball across their opponents' goal line to score a touchdown. At first sight, it might look like a disorganized free-for-all. But it is one of the most scientific of all team sports.

Outside the United States, the game is referred to as American football, to avoid confusion with soccer or other codes of football.

△ It looks like a brawl, as opposing sides battle for supremacy and no one seems to know where the ball is. But every man has a particular job to do in the overall plan, and teamwork is highly organized.

Professional teams have a squad of 45 players, with separate teams for offense, defense and special kicking situations.

Football is known as the "gridiron" game because of the field markings. It is the major national sport of the United States. It is played in schools and colleges and by professional teams.

In recent years its popularity has spread to other parts of the world, and the US professional game is followed worldwide on television.

A similar sport, played 12-a-side, is popular in Canada.

△ The quarterback throws a forward pass, one of the most exciting and spectacular features of the game.

The field of play

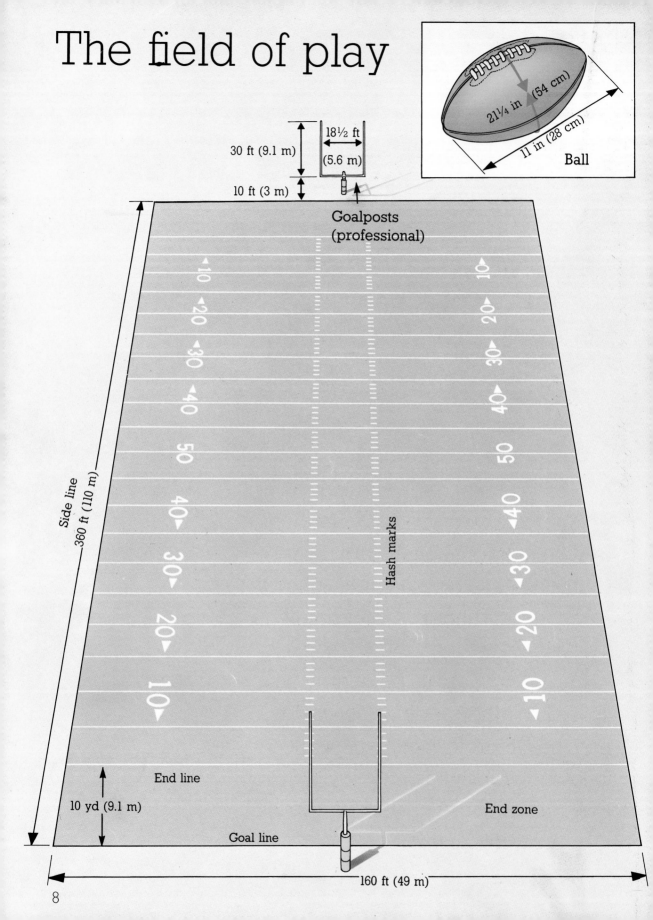

21¼ in (54 cm)

11 in (28 cm)

Ball

30 ft (9.1 m)

18½ ft (5.6 m)

10 ft (3 m)

Goalposts (professional)

10
20
30
40
50
40
30
20
10

Side line
360 ft (110 m)

Hash marks

End line

10 yd (9.1 m)

End zone

Goal line

160 ft (49 m)

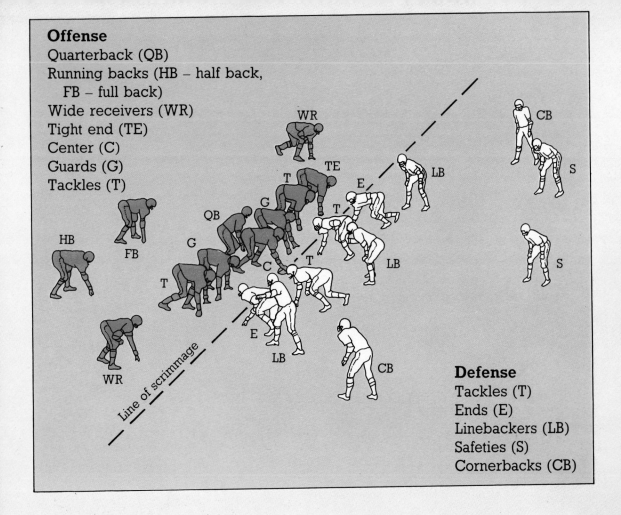

Offense
Quarterback (QB)
Running backs (HB – half back,
   FB – full back)
Wide receivers (WR)
Tight end (TE)
Center (C)
Guards (G)
Tackles (T)

Defense
Tackles (T)
Ends (E)
Linebackers (LB)
Safeties (S)
Cornerbacks (CB)

◀ **The field of play**

Lines cross the field of play every 5 yards, and are numbered every 10 yards. The numbers refer to the nearer goal line.

Hash marks, 1 yard apart, run the length of the field. In pro football, they are in line with the goalposts (as in the diagram). If a play finishes outside the hash marks, the next play starts with the ball on the nearest hash mark. Otherwise play restarts where the last play finished.

▲ **The line of scrimmage**

Most plays in football begin with a scrimmage. The teams face each other across an imaginery line, parallel to the yard lines, called the line of scrimmage. The line is as wide as the ball.

The diagram shows typical offensive and defensive formations. The offense must have at least seven players on or within 1 ft (30 cm) of the line. The defense may be positioned anywhere behind their side of the line. They usually have three or four men on the line.

More than just a game

Football is more than just a game. The players have been compared with gladiators, the trained warriors in armor who fought to the death to entertain the people of ancient Rome.

Football players go into "battle" with their own kind of armor – helmets and thickly padded uniforms. They are cheered on by thousands of fans and encouraged by cheerleaders and marching bands.

▽ With his arm guards already in place, a player (left) is helped on with his chest and shoulder padding.

Attached to the helmet (below) are a yellow face mask and a white chin guard. Hanging from the face mask is a mouthpiece that protects the teeth.

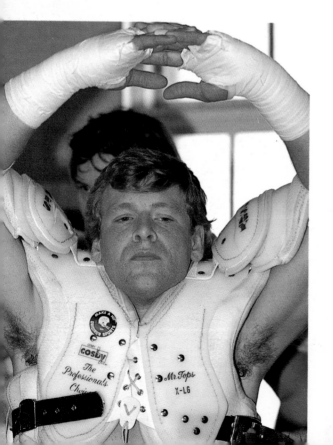

△ Cheerleaders are a traditional feature of the game. Wearing their team's colors, they dance and sing to encourage the players and rouse the fans.

▷ Fans enjoy a barbecue in the parking lot before a game. Called "tailgating," this is another tradition of football. Crowds are generally well behaved and good humored.

◁ The quarterback (No. 7) calls out signals before the start of a play. He is the onfield general, marshaling his men and carrying out his team's offensive strategy.

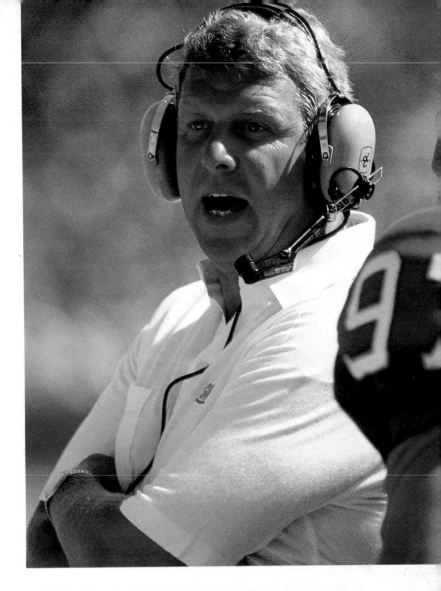

▷ The coach is the "field marshal." He plans the strategy and calls most of the plays. The coach uses players, coming on and off the field, to relay these plays to the quarterback.

▽ Seven officials ensure fair play – referee, umpire, head linesman, line judge, back judge, side judge and field judge.

Offense

The offense has four plays, called "downs," to advance the ball at least 10 yards. It does this by passing or running. If successful, in four or fewer downs, the offense has another "first down" and starts another series of plays.

If the offense fails to gain 10 yards, the opposing side wins possession of the ball. That side then brings on its offensive team for a first down.

△ Two teams face each other at the start of a first down, the offensive side, in possession of the ball, on the left, defense on the right. The red markers on the side line indicate the line of scrimmage (left) and the yardage needed to gain another first down.

The offense tries to progress toward the opponent's end zone on a series of first downs to score a touchdown, worth 6 points plus an extra point for a successful conversion kick.

On any down, the offense may attempt a field goal (3 points), scored by place-kicking the ball between the opponent's goalposts. If, on the fourth down, the offense is not within kicking distance of the goal, it may choose to punt.

▽ The start of a down is called the "snap." The center, with hand on ball, snaps it back to his quarterback, standing behind him. The quarterback, having instructed the team on the play before the start of the down, goes through the "starting count." This is in a simple code, confirming the play or making last-second changes and giving the signal for the center to snap the ball.

There are two main types of offensive move, the running play and the passing play. The quarterback may give the ball to a back, who tries to gain ground by running with the ball. Or he may run with the ball himself.

The quarterback may throw a forward pass to a receiver. He must throw it from behind the line of scrimmage, and only certain players, called "eligible receivers," are allowed to receive a forward pass.

▽ A running back dives over the goal line to score a touchdown. He does not have to ground the ball, but just break the "plane," an imaginary surface extending upward from the goal line. Running backs might run the length of the field to score a touchdown or, as in this case, just a yard or two. Their chief job is to gain yards by running, or "rushing," with the ball.

The eligible receivers are the two end players, called "wide receivers," the tight end and any player more than a yard behind the line at the snap.

On a passing play, the quarterback usually drops back to give his receivers time to advance upfield. They run planned "patterns" to deceive the defense and end up in the right spot for the quarterback's pass. A completed pass may win a first down or result in a touchdown.

△ A receiver goes up to catch a forward pass. He is in the end zone, so if he successfully completes the pass it will be a touchdown. For a completion, he must ground both feet within the field of play. The defender in front of him may catch the ball himself for an interception, or he may tip the ball away. But he must not impede the receiver or tackle him while the ball is in the air.

The center, the two guards and the two tackles are called the interior linemen. Their job is to protect the ball-carrier by blocking the defenders. They create gaps in the defense on running plays and provide a barrier for their quarterback on passing plays.

Blocking is legal obstruction. A blocker may use the upper part of his body, including his arms. But he must not spread his arms or use his hands to grab or hold.

▽ The offensive linemen in red shirts attempt to block the defensive linemen and prevent them from breaking through. Not all blocking takes place on or around the line of scrimmage. A player may protect a rusher by "running interference," keeping himself between the ball-carrier and would-be tacklers.

Defense

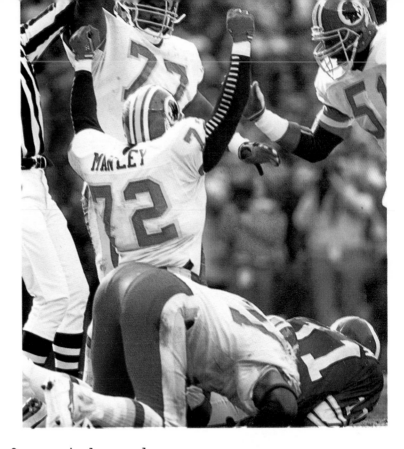

The play of the defense is largely dictated by what kind of moves the offense makes.

The defensive ends and tackles are usually the heaviest men in the squad. Their job is to break up the offensive block on passing plays and stand firm on running plays. The defensive players usually have no more than a split second to decide whether to advance or stand their ground. So they need brains as well as brawn to read the play and react to it.

▽ A triumph for the defensive lineman. The quarterback (in blue) has just been tackled before he could pass the ball. This is called sacking. The offense still has the ball, but usually loses considerable yardage on the play. If a sack, or any successful tackle of the ball-carrier, occurs in his own end zone, a safety, worth 2 points, is scored by the defending side.

The linebackers are the middle unit of the defense. They must be strong yet fast and possess quick minds.

They must react quickly to offensive moves, and counter them, ready to tackle the running back or force their way through to a passing quarterback. They may also have to drop back to protect against a pass.

△ Lawrence Taylor of the New York Giants, one of the all-time great linebackers, stops an opposing ball-carrier in his tracks.

The last line of defense, called the secondary, is usually made up of two safeties and two cornerbacks. Also called defensive backs, they are generally the smallest men on the team.

Defensive backs must be fast and sure in the tackle. The cornerbacks mark the wide receivers. The safeties defend against long passes and running plays through the middle, and support the cornerbacks.

▽ A defensive back tackles the ball-carrier and causes a fumble. This is a loss of possession by the offense. If the defense manages to grab the ball, it is called a turnover and possession goes to the defending side.

Defensive backs often bring about a turnover by inter-cepting a pass to a wide receiver. The defense can run a ball back on a turnover and even score a touchdown.

Special teams

Special teams are the men brought on for the various kicking plays – punts, kick-offs, and field goal and extra point, or conversion, attempts.

Both teams bring on these special squads, for kicking and defending against the kick. A team has two specialist kickers, one for punting and one for place-kicks. Other members of these teams include blockers, runners, kick returners, a player to snap the ball and one to catch and hold it for the kicker.

▷ The center snaps the ball back for the holder, often a reserve quarterback, to place for the kicker. Place-kicks are for field goals or conversions. The ball is snapped back from the scrimmage position, which for the extra point is on the 2-yard line. In some grades of football, the offense can go for a further 2-point touchdown instead of the conversion.

▽ The defense tries to break through to rush the kicker.

▷A punter goes for height as well as distance. A team will punt on the last down when not within field goal distance. They can send two wide men upfield as soon as the ball is snapped. The rest of the punt coverage team has to wait until the ball is kicked before going upfield. The object is to keep the punt return to a minimum or even recover possession.

◁A plastic tee is used to hold the ball for a kick-off, which takes place to start each half and by the scoring team after a score. The kicking team takes the kick-off from its 35-yard line and tries to kick the ball as far as possible and keep the return to a minimum.

The NFL and Super Bowl

Professional football in the United States is run by the National Football League, or NFL. Games in the NFL are televised to many countries, and the standard of playing is far higher than anywhere else in the world.

The NFL is made up of the American Football Conference and the National Football Conference. Each has 14 teams playing in three divisions.

△ New York Giants players on the side line. NFL teams have squads of 45. Most of the players come up through the colleges. After each season there is a college draft, in which the NFL teams choose players. The idea of the draft is to even up playing strengths. The team with the worst record in the NFL gets first choice in each round, the Super Bowl winners last choice.

The NFL regular season lasts from mid-September to the end of December, each team playing 16 games. The teams in a division play each other twice (home and away), and also play teams in other divisions of their conference and teams in the other conference.

At the end of the regular season, the team with the best won-lost record in each division goes to the play-offs.

△ Brian Brennan, wide receiver of the Cleveland Browns, catches a pass in the end zone for a touchdown in an American Football Conference play-off game, despite the attentions of Indianapolis cornerback Terry Wright.

The two teams with the next best record in each conference play off for a "wild card" entry to the play-offs. In each conference there are then semi-finals and a final, to determine the conference champions.

On the last Sunday in January, the two conference champions play each other in the Super Bowl game. The winners are the NFL champions.

▽ Washington Redskins quarterback Doug Williams turns with the ball during the 1988 Super Bowl against the Denver Broncos. The Super Bowl is the climax of the NFL season.

The story of football

Origins

Many ancient civilizations played games in which a ball was kicked. The various football codes as we know them today had their origins in Britain. Soccer began to take shape in the early 1800s. In 1823, when a boy at Rugby School, in England, picked up a ball and ran with it, rugby football was born.

△ Football at Rugby School, England, where the rugby code was born.

A mixture of two codes

Both football codes, soccer and rugby, found their way across the Atlantic. Out of them evolved a distinctive American game, called football in the United States and American football elsewhere.

School and college football

As in Britain, the game in the United States developed in schools and colleges. By 1905, however, the blocking and tackling had become dangerously violent and players were kicking and punching each other. Several deaths had occurred on the field.

President Theodore Roosevelt called for a complete reform of the game or he would abolish it. Walter Camp, who had devised the scrimmage and the snap, was again the man to come up with new ideas. He brought in neutral officials and encouraged a more open game by making more scope for the forward pass. The four downs in 10 yards system was introduced.

△ From 1906 to 1910 criss-cross markings divided the field into 5-yard squares.

The professional game

Professional football, which began in the mid-1890s, did not become properly organized until

△ The Rose Bowl in Pasadena, California, scene of the major college game between eastern and western universities since 1902.

1920. An association was formed which in 1922 became known as the National Football League (NFL). The NFL has seen many changes over the years and rival leagues have come and gone, but it remains the ruling body of professional football in the United States.

The national sport

College football had long been popular nationwide in the US before professional football began to increase its following in the 1950s with the advent of television. A big breakthrough for the pro game came in 1958, when some 50 million viewers saw the Baltimore Colts beat the New York Giants in a thrilling overtime match for the championship. Within 20 years, the Super Bowl, first held in 1967, took over from baseball's World Series as the most watched sports event on television. Football could reasonably claim to be the national sport of the United States.

The spread of the game

Television has also been responsible for the recent spread of American football around the world. Sportsmen in other countries began to take up the code and many countries formed their own leagues.

In 1986, two leading NFL teams played a pre-season game at Wembley Stadium, England. This has become an annual event, known as the American Bowl. So football had returned to the country that gave the world its first football codes.

△ The Denver Broncos play the Los Angeles Rams at Wembley Stadium, England, in the 1987 American Bowl.

Facts and records

△ Quarterback Doug Williams, Redskins hero and record-breaker in the 1988 Super Bowl.

Redskin record-breakers

The Washington Redskins smashed several Super Bowl records when they beat Denver 42–10 in the 1988 championship game. These included 340 yards gained passing by quarterback Doug Williams, 204 yards rushing by running back Timmy Smith and 193 yards receiving by wide receiver Ricky Sanders. Washington's 6 touchdowns also broke the Super Bowl record.

Television attraction

Of the ten most watched TV programs of all time in the United States, eight have been Super Bowls. At the top of the list is Super Bowl XX, seen by 127 million viewers on January 26, 1986. The only other programs in the top ten are a $M*A*S*H$ special and an episode of the dramatic series, *Roots*.

Rushing records

Chicago Bears running back Walter Payton retired at the end of the 1987 season with ten NFL records. In 13 seasons as a professional, he had gained 16,726 yards in regular season play, over 4,000 yards more than the previous record, and scored a record 110 touchdowns. He also held the record for the most yardage gained in a game, with 275 yards against Minnesota in 1977.

△ Chicago running back Walter Payton, rusher supreme.

Glossary

Down
One of a series of plays an offense has in which to gain 10 yards.

Draft
The method by which college players are allotted to professional teams.

Eligible receivers
The offensive players who are permitted to catch a forward pass.

Fumble
Loss of possession by a player by accident or from a tackle. The ball can be recovered by any player on the field.

Hash marks
The two series of short lines running the length of the field. Play always restarts on or between the two sets of marks.

Interception
The catching of a pass by a defensive player. A player making an interception may run with the ball and his side keeps possession.

Punt
A kick taken, usually on a fourth down, when the offense cannot risk going for a first down and is too far away for a field goal attempt.

Rushing
Running with the ball to gain yardage.

Sacking
Tackling the quarterback behind the line of scimmage for a loss of yardage.

Safety
One of the central players in the last line of the defense. Also, a score, worth 2 points to the defense, when the ball-carrier is tackled in his own end zone.

Scrimmage
The play that starts each down, with the two sides facing each other across the line of scrimmage.

Snap
The method of starting play at a scrimmage. The center flips the ball back between his legs.

Turnover
Change of possession brought about by a fumble or an interception.

Index